Safe Passage

THE "PARENT 2 PARENT" MENTORING PROGRAM

RICHARD J. DELANEY, PH.D.
ILLUSTRATIONS BY TERRY McNERNEY

Published by:

Wood 'N' Barnes Publishing & Distribution
2717 NW 50th
Oklahoma City, OK 73112
(405) 942-6812

Illustrations by Terry McNerney
Cover Art by Blu Designs.
Copyediting & Design by Ramona Cunningham.

Printed in the United States of America
Oklahoma City, Oklahoma
ISBN # 1-885473-32-x

To order copies of this book, please call:
Jean Barnes Books
800-678-0621

ACKNOWLEDGEMENTS

I would like to thank the following individuals and programs for their essential assistance in the publication of this guidebook for adoptive parents:

The Kellogg Foundation and Families For Kids;
The Montana Department of Public Health and Human Services,
The Adoption Exchange and The Casey Family Program, Missoula.
Specifically, I would like to acknowledge the foresight of Mary Olson
of DPHHS for design of the workshops on Parent 2 Parent Mentoring;
the support of Joe Loos of The Casey Family Program
in setting up the pilot mentoring project;
the overall impetus of the Kellogg foundation in promoting
permanence for children in Montana;
and the generosity of The Adoption Exchange in sharing training materials
prepared in its "Permanency Through Adoption" series in Colorado
(funded by a grant from the State of Colorado, Department of Human Services).

Most importantly, I want to express my gratitude to
Norm & Bonnie and Chris & Glen
for their willingness to become guinea pigs, to try out the mentoring idea, to make
it real, and to open up their lives for scrutiny and examination.
If they had not excelled in implementing this notion of mentoring, we would
perhaps not have endured.

This book is dedicated to the memory of Bonnie Evans,
an extraordinary woman, wife, mother and mentor.
Proceeds from sales of this book and the related videotape are deposited in
a trust account for special needs adopted children and their families.

A NOTE FROM THE PUBLISHER ⚷

We live what we learn.

Children of all ages (adults, too!) emulate the actions and behaviors of those that surround them. Being a positive and appropriate role model for someone is the greatest gift that you can give. Modeling positive behaviors, being a living example of good decision making, and exemplifying compassion and empathy are the focus of quality mentors, parents and human beings.

With your review of this curriculum, you are well on the way to providing "safe passage" not only to the children in your care but to the foster and adoptive parents that are to be mentored as well. The "Parent 2 Parent" video program, along with the healthy and well-rounded review by Dr. Delaney in this text "Safe Passage," will join his other works as "required resources" for foster and adoptive families.

Adding a calming voice and perspective to the chaos that is child placement, Dr. Delaney lends an awareness of the possibilities available to those who sometimes feel lost in the pressured decisions that alter the futures of children. Written in his usual humorous yet insightful and intelligent style, Dr. Delaney offers clear examples and practical illustrations to bring the message of mentoring to foster care.

David Wood
Publisher

CONTENTS ⚷

*We hope to provide safe passage for both child and parent(s)
through the adventures of adopting.*

FOREWORD

O *ur zeal to place children in adoptive homes must be matched by our fervor to support those homes after placement. Only then can we provide safe passage for parents and children through the ofttimes rugged terrain of special needs adoption.*

At last adoption has become a national priority. What's more, foster children with special needs will be adopted in greater numbers following passage of the Adoption and Safe Families Act, 1997. Congratulations are in order for those whose quest to secure adoptive homes for foster children has culminated in a re-dedication to permanency. Congratulations truly are deserved. However, congratulatory wishes must not lead to complacency. Yes, increasing adoption rates are reducing the numbers of children who wait, but we must follow with post-adoptive services that ensure successful adoptions. We should not just find good families for needy children, complete permanency and exit stage left. Our goal should be to provide loving families which experience the "successful adventure" of raising a special needs adopted child. Through the "Parent 2 Parent Mentoring Program," described herein, we hope to provide safe passage for both child and parents through the adventure of adopting.

This present book, "Safe Passage," and the pilot project (Parent 2 Parent) it summarizes, grow out of a belief in supporting parents in the loving struggle, the challenging journey of a special needs adoption. Thus, this project began by providing support to adopting parents, e.g., Chris and Glen, newcomers to adoption who live in remote Montana with their four troubled, adopted kids. With the nearest support group an hour's drive away (in good weather) and an eternity away in a January blizzard, they needed intense support close by. But, who had the experience to offer specific help to Chris and Glen on their journey with their children? Who could offer emotional support and guidance? Enter Norm and Bonnie, seasoned foster parents who, by divine providence, lived within ten miles of Chris and Glen. (Ten miles is a walk around the block in rural Montana.) Their role with Chris and Glen evolved from sounding board to emotional backers to advice givers; and eventually it became more than that. Ultimately, Norm and Bonnie were knowledgable friends helping to assure "safe passage" to parents and children whom they truly knew and cared for, and whose challenging journey they intimately understood.

It is hoped that this book will provide a glimpse at what is possible when experienced adoptive parents, that is, seasoned travelers, come into close contact with relatively inexperienced parents who have just begun their journey with troubled adopted children. It is also hoped that this book will offer helpful tips on the provision (e.g. through mentoring) of safe passage to adopting parents and adopted children alike.

Richard J. Delaney
Kalaheo, Island of Kauai
Hawaii
January, 2000

INTRODUCTION

When I think about foster and adoptive parents, three stories pop into my mind. The first was told by a comedian who pointed out, "Parenting is like a bath. At first it's pretty comfy, but pretty soon it ain't so hot!"

The second story involved a man whose circus job was to be shot from a cannon. John, "The Human Cannon Ball," was tired of the circus and decided to quit. The circus owner was truly upset and asked him, "Where are we going to find someone of your caliber?"

And the third story had to do with a foster parent who showed up at the counselor's office with her troubled child and said, "Excuse me, but I was wondering if you could help me out." "Certainly," said the counselor, "Go right out that exit."

Here's how these three stories apply here:

- As most parents who are fostering or adopting troubled children already know, parenting can turn out to be "not so hot"—especially when the parents get a lukewarm or even cold response from the child they are trying to help, to reach, to parent.

- Like John, "The Human Cannon Ball," many parents feel like they've been shot out of a gun once too of-

"I now realize that a large part of parenting is simple survival. I put on my combat gear each day and collapse each night in peace with the knowledge that my family has survived another day." Patricia Robertson

1

*Many children are adrift in the system,
floating without direction until adopted.*

ten. The job of parenting troubled or challenging children produces a level of stress with which many parents are unfamiliar. Even if they are the right "caliber" for the job, it's tough to keep them hanging in there day-in-and-day-out dreading the next swift trip out of the end of a cannon.

•Unfortunately, many parents who seek help cannot find what they need. Either they connect with professionals who don't understand their unique situation, or they find helpers who feel out of their depth with the level of disturbance presented by the children. While few parents are actually kicked out of offices, they are often referred on to others, who refer them on to still others.

The overall hope for mentoring is that we help bring to the foster or adoptive family a better understanding of the child's past and how it impacts everybody around him; that we try to inject more enjoyment and pleasure into the sometimes laborious task of parenting troubled kids; and that we offer a vision of a brighter future for the family and child.

"Love cures people, the ones who receive love and the ones who give it, too."
Karl A. Menninger

MENTORING

THE BASICS:
With the passage of the Adoption and Safe Families Act of 1997, we anticipate an increase in the adoptions of special

It is not the intent of this project to make look-alike clones out of mentors and mentees.

needs children, children who are older, who have emotional or physical problems and/or who are of a minority group. (We will discuss special needs further ahead.) In some instances, individuals with no prior experience with these children will agree to take them into their homes, to adopt, and to provide permanence. "Parent 2 Parent" mentoring is one avenue through which we offer support to new families who take on the challenge of adopting a special needs child.

MENTORING DEFINED:

In Greek mythology, Mentor was the teacher of Telmachus, the son of Odysseus. Mentoring is defined as: teaching, tutoring or coaching provided by a trusted confidant. For our purposes, mentoring is the pairing of a veteran foster or adoptive family with a novice family to offer support and advice.

"mentor n. Experienced adviser and supporter."

"trust n. Confidence in and reliance on good qualities, especially fairness, truth, honor or ability."

OBJECTIVES OF MENTORING:

The overall objectives of mentoring are to stabilize, overcome isolation, engender hope and provide safe passage for child and family. Mentoring also validates, advocates, informs, advises, interprets, calibrates expectations, and supports emotionally.

MATCHING OF MENTORING GROUPS:

Matching mentor and mentee is more art than science. That is, we can never tell in advance whether two families will complement each other. In instances where parents have

🔑 *"The precise nature of each mentor partnership must be allowed to take on its own personality, its own character, and some of its own functions."*

known each other from support groups, from the neighborhood or from foster parent associations, it may be simple to engender a partnership.

Each mentor/mentee partnership is unique. While mentors should possess traits such as compassion, understanding, sharing, humor, and objectivity, they are unique individuals whose greatest asset is themselves. Further, the precise nature of each mentor partnership must be allowed to take on its own personality, its own character, and some of its own functions. It is not the intent of this project to make look-alike clones out of mentors and mentees.

MENTORING - A FORM OF ON-THE-JOB TRAINING:

An experienced caseworker reported recently that 50% of foster parents burn out within the first year of caring for foster children. That is, oftentimes the first child placed with a new foster family is also the last child ever placed. A third worker from the agency adoption unit admitted that first-time adoptive parents are being given troubled, highly challenging children or sibling groups without adequate preparation and follow-up support. "We truly want to help each individual foster or adoptive family, but the money is simply not there to do it right!" lamented this worker, who went on, "We are so desperate for families, for permanent and even temporary homes, that if we conclude that the parents have a pulse and a permanent address, we have to go for it!"

As mentioned above, too many first time foster and adoptive parents drop out or burnout soon after the placement of the disturbed child. And, it appears that there is very little time to prevent burnout. Additionally, there is a very small window of opportunity to train parents to handle things which cause the burnout: e.g. the child's attachment issues, acting-out behavior, targeting of the foster/adoptive mother, etc. The window opens when the honeymoon ends (when the insights occur about how troubled the child is), and the window slams shut when the family feels discouraged, overwhelmed and totally inadequate. The window may be open for a year, a month, or a few days.

Very few adopting parents can be properly trained beforehand for the challenging, sometimes flummoxing task of adopting a special needs child due to the following:

1) Prospective parents are typically and understandably in the stage of infatuation. That is, they are thrilled by the notion of having a child and they are often idealistic about what they can accomplish with the child;

2) They may not have the life experience with a child which would permit them to completely grasp what others are trying to convey to them about troubled youngsters; and

3) They harbor one or more myths about adopting the troubled child. (More about myths later.)

☞ "I appreciate the fact that kids come complete with self-recharging batteries. What I don't understand is why they come without instruction manuals. And now that I think about it, what about guarantees?"
Patricia Robertson

Adoption can bring together some unlikely combinations.

SPECIAL NEEDS ADOPTIONS:

Many of the children who will be the ultimate beneficiaries of the "Parent 2 Parent" mentoring program have been labeled "special needs" adoptive children. Many have had past placements in foster care, group homes, even residential treatment settings and/or hospital facilities. Special needs adoptive children possess one or more of the following factors:

- A history of maltreatment, abuse, neglect, sexual exploitation;
- A checkered chronology of multiple placements, formal and informal;
- Ethnic or racial minority status;
- Older age at time of availability for adoption, e.g. over six;
- They are part of a packaged deal, e.g., a sibling group up for adoption together;
- Documented medical problems;
- Emotional, behavioral or mental disorder;
- A physical or developmental disability.

Many of the factors listed above impact the child in ways that threaten his or her capacity to adapt to an adoptive family without assistance.

☛ *"Anything will give up its secrets if you love it enough."* George Washington Carver

OVERVIEW OF THE BOOK:

Chapter One addresses the characteristic problems of troubled adopted children. Many parents are unprepared for problem behaviors such as lying, stealing, hoarding of food, and cruelty to animals. This chapter lists thirteen common behavior problems found in some special needs adopted children.

Chapter Two focuses upon the impact felt by the adoptive family when raising a troubled adopted child. Most new adoptive parents are unprepared for how dramatically life can change within the family following the placement of a disturbed child in the home.

Chapter Three outlines eight common myths held by those who adopt special needs children.

Chapter Four summarizes the mentoring task of providing advice. Most mentees need someone's input—input they can trust. This chapter addresses areas in which advice-giving can be most helpful to new adoptive parents.

Chapter Five addresses the role of mentors when an adoption disruption or dissolution is possible or has already occurred.

Chapter Six describes the process of mentoring when there is a need for concrete, specific strategies to be employed with children in the adoptive home.

NOTES ✒ NOTES ✒ NOTES ✒ NOTES

Many adopted children have endured life on a psychological roller coaster.
Six Flags over Sodom and Gomorrah.

CHAPTER ONE

TODAY'S TROUBLED CHILDREN

Note: While mentors are usually cognizant of it, many mentees may be unaware and unprepared for how troubled some adopted children are. This chapter briefly describes common behavioral problems demonstrated by disturbed adopted children.

🔑 *"Early abuse and neglect lead children to erect complex barricades on the most fragile of foundations."*

An adopted eight-year-old girl had the unappetizing problem of soiling herself several times per day. When efforts to help her control this problem were increased, the child smeared feces in her hair and ground it into the carpet. The adoptive mother commented sardonically, "It's hard to live down wind from this child."

A ten-year-old adopted boy was described as stubborn, contrary, oppositional, and "defiant around the clock." He had a list of diagnoses a mile long: ODD, ADHD, OCD, PTSD, and RAD (Reactive Attachment Disorder). On or off medication he acted much the same: he would argue with a fence post, refuse to obey and comply, and generally resist authority at home or school. He battled constantly for control in the family, which exhausted the adoptive mother and infuriated the father. "Our life is a war zone," they lamented.

A fifteen-year-old adopted boy, who looked more like an eleven- or twelve-year-old, exhausted his parents with unfathomable needs. Raised by a hypochondriachal birth mother who alter-

Many abused children are hypervigilant...
alert to physical and emotional dangers around them.

nated between doting on the boy and demanding slavish attention from him, he learned to expect intense and unending interactions with her. He was either the recipient or provider of massive quantities of attention. In the three foster placements following his mother's death, his clinging behavior with each successive foster mother triggered disruption of each placement in turn. Once placed in an adoptive family, this needy teen-with-no-boundaries shunned the adoptive father, exclusively focusing demands on an increasingly drained adoptive mother.

You may already be well aware that today's foster children are quite disturbed. It's not surprising that these youngsters, most of whom have been victims of chronic maltreatment, abuse, neglect and/or sexual exploitation, are still reeling from the negative effects long after they come to live with good families. Sadly, many of these children cannot bear to receive the very things they need most: solid family life and dependable love from parents. Ironically, almost mysteriously, many kids seem to make themselves unlovable. Tragically some children seem to go out of their way to keep others from caring about them and from wanting to even be around them.

"Victory is not won in miles, but in inches. Win a little now, hold your ground and later win a little more."
Louis L'Amour

Much of what makes troubled foster and adopted children unlovable is the pattern of problem behaviors they unleash in their new homes, schools, and communities. The list of possible troublesome and troubling behavior problems is long and includes the following:

1. Lying ... For some children lying is a reflex. Their motto is: a lie, not the truth, will set you free.

"Loving is the most creative force in the universe."
Peter McWilliams

15

*Other children enter adoptive homes like tyrants,
dictators in search of control over family life.*

2. Stealing ... Petty theft, shop-lifting and even grand larceny are not uncommon in troubled foster and adopted youngsters. This problem usually suggests a history of neglect and an attitude of entitlement.

3. Fire-Setting ... Whether a product of foolish match play or calculated pyromania, fire-setting may have very serious implications. In the case of pyromania, anger is often at the root of the problem.

4. Sexual Acting-Out ... With an estimated 3/4ths of children coming into foster care having been sexually abused, sexual acting out and obsessiveness are commonplace. Sometimes there are no prior reports of the child's sexualized behavior, nor have there been, in some cases, substantiated incidents of sexual victimization.

5. Opposition or Defiant Behavior ... This behavior may be nearly universal in today's troubled adopted children.

6. Cruelty to Pets ... Sadistic behavior toward animals, well beyond poor judgment or youthful experimentation, may be a scary harbinger of how the child may relate in the future toward harmless beings.

7. Aggressive/Assaultive Behavior ... Most troubled adopted children show problems with anger management. They either rigidly control it, or they vacillate between over- and under-control of anger.

> 🔑 *"No matter how big and tough a problem may be, get rid of confusion by taking one little step toward a solution."*
> George F. Nordenhold

> 🔑 *"We can do no great things–only small things with great love."*
> Mother Teresa

Parental children have often raised themselves, younger children and even infirmed or needy parents.

8. Temper Tantrums ... Temper tantrums often connote anger not directly targeting other individuals. The child head-bangs, tears up his room, or stomps down the hallway. In any of these instances, the child usually is reacting to frustration, disappointment, or the word "no" from an authority figure. Serious tantrums, depending upon the age of the child, typically point to overall emotional immaturity.

9. Vandalism/Destruction of Property ... Frequently, a sign of solitary protest, vandalism indicates a certain vengeful streak in the child.

10. Hoarding Food ... Usually an indication of early physical or emotional deprivation and neglect, stealing and hiding food suggests that the child fears the return of starvation conditions. He also assumes that no one can be counted on to nurture him.

11. Indiscriminate Attachment ... When the child shows no sense of belonging, he commonly turns to strangers. He displays a sad blurring of emotional relationships.

12. Lack of Remorse ... Guilt, conscience and true remorse are often absent or limited in troubled adopted children who were brought up in an amoral early environment. True remorse is predicated upon an attachment to a loved one.

13. Provoking Anger in Others ... Irritating, antagonizing, and provoking others to anger suggest that

"What appears to us as the impossible may be simply the untried."
Seyyed Hossein Nasr

☛ *"To accomplish great things, we must not only act, but also dream; not only plan, but also believe."* Anatole France

the child feels safer when others vocalize his silent anger for him.

(Other behavior problems include: insatiable neediness, chaotic behavior, and fundamental love-hate issues with mother figures. More complete listings of common behavioral problems are found in *Fostering Changes: Treating Attachment Disordered Foster Children,* and *Raising Cain: Caring For Troubled Youngsters/Repairing Our Troubled System.*)

While few children show all of the above-listed behavior problems, the presence of even one such problem can destabilize an adoptive family.

Note: Many of the problem behaviors listed above can be traced to medical, neurological, or psychiatric disorders. Others may be directly linked to the child's experience of maltreatment, which may result in the formation of an attachment disorder. This disorder is marked by, among other things, significant troubles in making and sustaining normal emotional connections with caretakers. Appendix A provides in table format the "attachment continuum," which is a way of understanding a child's relative position vis-a-vis attachment.

QUESTIONS TO PONDER OR DISCUSS 🔑

1. What would you add to the list of problems observed in some troubled adopted children?

2. Do the children you have adopted display any of the problem behaviors described here?

3. Were you prepared for the problems your child(ren) displayed?

4. What accounts for these problem behaviors?

5. Select a problem behavior. How might you handle this problem behavior?

NOTES ✒ NOTES ✒ NOTES ✒ NOTES

NOTES ⚏ NOTES ⚏ NOTES ⚏ NOTES

*Today's adoptive parents constantly juggle child care, career and domestic tasks.
A special needs adoptive child can add stress to an already charged life.*

IMPACT ON ADOPTIVE FAMILY MEMBERS

Note: Most new adopting parents are unprepared for the dramatic impact of raising a disturbed, special needs child. This chapter will describe aspects of negative impact within the adoptive home.

🗝 *"The sixty-four thousand dollar question is, 'Will the adoptive parents reach this troubled child before the child gets to them?'"*

T*he Smith's birth children kept secret from their parents the fact that they had barricaded their bedroom doors on a nightly basis. Due to threats of physical harm from Bobby, their newly adopted brother, the children cowered behind locked doors.*

Not much is written on the impact of raising troubled children. Yet, it is indisputable: raising a troubled child can be hazardous to your emotional balance, to the stability of your marriage, and to the psychological and sometimes physical well-being of your other children.

Some children tremble at the mention of the "A" word - adoption. Especially if they have failed in previous adoptive attempts, or if their allegiances to birth family collides with the idea of adoption. Although some youngsters may find the concept of adoption highly appealing, the day-to-day reality of an adoptive family can turn out to be confusing, threatening, and even repugnant to other children. These children are often ill-equipped to live in the intimate embrace

Adoption often involves balancing the needs of one consuming child against that of other less troubled children.

of close ties and close quarters. They feel such conflicting emotions about mothers, fathers, and/or other children that they torpedo the very life raft which could carry them to safety. With the disruptive bad habits and/or inappropriate roles they may have acquired, their arrival in the adoptive home can produce a great deal of turmoil. As a result, the parenting family can become discouraged and sink under the weight of the child's negative influence on them.

Which reminds me of a story. A mother found her three-year-old boy playing with a box of bullets. She was shocked to find that he had swallowed a couple. Panic stricken, she sped him to the local hospital. The ER doctor examined the boy thoroughly, fed him a heavy duty laxative, and released him to his mother with these instructions. "Take him home and keep him quiet. And whatever you do, don't point him at anybody for the next few hours!" As with this little boy, many of our foster and adopted children have swallowed a lot of things they shouldn't have. And, when it comes out, these kids are often pointed directly at the adoptive family.

Here are some of the central issues which may emerge:

1. The Scapemom in Your Home … The adoptive (or foster) mother bears the sins of all previous mothers who have loved-and-left or failed the child in some way.

2. Imported Pathology of the Child and How It Can Be Contagious … That is, the child brings emotional baggage into your family, which he unpacks in your home. The baggage can sometimes have a stronger

"Life itself is a strange mixture. We have to take it as it is, try to understand it and then better it."
Rabindranath Tagore

The scapemom often receives mixed love/hate signals from the troubled adopted child. These are come hither/go yonder messages.

influence on you than your effect on the child.

3. The Marital Schism ... Fathers and mothers rarely experience the disturbed child in the same way—at least initially. Primarily it is the mother who experiences more defiance, anger, and ambivalence from the child. The father, in a more revered position, experiences the child much less negatively.

4. The 99% Child and the Undernourishment of the Nuclear Family ... Some special needs adoptive children are so needy and time-consuming that they claim all the care-giving. Very little is left for others.

5. Idealization of the Abusers ... Ironically, the child often canonizes the memory of those who have maltreated him in terrible, chronic ways. At the same time, the child devalues those who have committed themselves to him or her.

6. Revolving Scapegoat Behavior ... It seems like a law of nature that if there are several children in the home, they take turns at being the most challenging and disturbed. As one child improves, others take his place.

7. Common Reactions in the Re-Enactment Scheme ... The most common reactions which adoptive parents report is feeling swept up in a replay of the child's past. Feelings of anger, the desire to reject, and despair can sweep over parents who live with the troubled adopted child.

Reducing mother burnout is essential to successful adoptions.

8. The Challenge of Parenting a Self-Parented Child … When children have learned to take care of themselves or to raise themselves without adult involvement, they become perpetually self-parenting. While many of them will accept the accouterments of adoption, e.g. a roof over one's head, three meals a day, and so on, they are disinterested in having a true parent-child relationship, at least initially.

9. Extended Family Problems … Involvement with mentors is quite important, given the common reaction of extended family members to the adopting parents. Commonly, extended family members underestimate or minimize the child's disturbance and react critically to the adoptive parents attempts at managing the child in their home.

10. Going from Saint to Sinner … Society–friends, neighbors, and the community at large–generally are quite positive about others adopting children. Indeed, many adopting parents receive praise and "how do you do it?" accolades from others, for a time. However, when the disturbed adopted children continue to act out in the community, then others criticize the adoptive parents for not fixing the child quickly, or even for making the child worse.

11. Isolation … Many adoptive parents find themselves losing social contacts that they had in the past, before the adoption. They also find that others cannot truly understand what they are experiencing.

"Not merely what we do, but what we try to do and why, are the true interpreters of what we are."
C. H. Woodward

12. From Honeymoon to Burn Out ... There are predictable stages adoptive parents pass through, first feeling that others have exaggerated, later feeling that others have underestimated the child's problems.

13. Grieving the Loss of Life as It Was ... Blessings and benefits aside, taking on a special needs child may dramatically alter marital and family relationships in both positive and less positive ways. Loss of the original nuclear family is a central concern.

QUESTIONS TO PONDER OR DISCUSS ∼

1. Discuss how adoption has impacted your family life.

2. Has the child elicited strong emotions and reactions from you?

3. How is your view of the child different from that of your spouse, other family members or friends?

NOTES ⟞ NOTES ⟞ NOTES ⟞ NOTES

CHAPTER THREE

MYTHS ABOUT ADOPTING

"Becoming a parent demands a hefty dose of infatuation and a temporary state of insanity. For all the rational explanations for why we do it, becoming a parent—even deciding to become a parent—often requires a hopefully fleeting condition of mental imbalance. We resort to reason, but, in the end, the decision is more emotional leap than logical step. It's idealism over realism. And in the end, choosing to parent is less about reason and more about myth."

➤◇ *"Choosing to parent is less about reason and more about myth."*

Note: Before experiencing a special needs adoption or prior to living with a troubled child, most parents harbor certain myths.

P roducing a child or taking on the raising of a child takes motivation, and it also takes a leap of faith, a mandatory idealism, a necessary bravado. Further, it takes reliance on myths, some of which can get us into trouble.

One author alleged that all humans are guided by three myths: infallibility of opinion, irresistability of charm, and immortality of being. That is, we are always right, down right appealing, and will never die. (As a parent, one quickly learns that he/she is never right, sometimes unappealing, and prays

myth n. A fiction or half-truth. ➤◇

for premature death. So much for those three myths!)

As parents or parents-to-be, myths abound: we believe we can do it, we suspect it'll be full of wonder, and we truly think that we can do it well. Although we may acknowledge doubts before hand, at onset most parents radiate optimism and confidence.

Eight of the most common parenting myths held by prospective and typically first time adoptive parents are listed below:

1. You Must Be Kidding. Children can't really be that disturbed.

2. Not In My House. WE won't have those problems in OUR home.

3. Love Is Enough. Once these kids are exposed to our brand of love, real love from a devoted parent, they will thrive.

4. Kids Is Kids? If you have parented other kids you can parent these kids.

5. The One Year for One Year Rule. For each traumatic year, the child will require one year to heal.

6. You Need to Handle Your Own Problems. Seeking outside help is for wimps.

7. Adoption Finalization Will Always Change the Child

☞ "All generalizations are false, including this one."
Alexander Chase

for the Better.

8. We Can Change All Kids.

Let's look at each of these myths in detail, since they have such an important impact on parenting, preparing for it, and reaching out for assistance after we have begun the journey.

1. You've Got To Be Kidding

New adoptive parents when first provided information on a child with emotional and behavioral problems, simply can't believe it. A child disturbed by the age of four! Psshaw! A child who might refuse their love! Poppycock! A youngster who has already developed entrenched behavior problems! Indeed!

"The first problem for all of us, men and women, is not to learn, but to unlearn."
Gloria Steinem

Adults who have not previously fostered or adopted troubled children often minimize, disregard, or totally disbelieve reports about children's problems. This leads many parents to believe, "We don't need any help!" However, in short order, they often feel, "We (and our adopted child) are totally beyond help!"

2. Not In My Home

Even when the adopted child's history reveals that previous homes have been disrupted, that the child has become unmanageable, and that others have given up on him, new parents assume that in their home it will be categorically different. However, they often are categorically wrong!

3. LOVE IS ENOUGH

A common misconception held by new parents is the belief that the reported problems of the child will respond to love. However, devotion, affection and concern for the child often fall short with troubled children when not augmented with an array of other parenting skills and strategies.

A related myth is that if the parents and family offer their love to a child that it will be accepted, appreciated and reciprocated. In actuality, though, too many adoptive parents drive the wrong way down a one-way street, on a collision course with oncoming rejection from the child.

4. KIDS IS KIDS

A most insidious and counterproductive myth held by many about special needs adoptive children is that all children are fundamentally alike. Accordingly, how we relate to and help a special needs child is identical to the average child. Neighbors or relatives of the adoptive parents often endorse this myth, viewing reported problems as identical to the typical child. For example, if the adoptive parent reports, "He is so full of anger." The response is often, "Well, **all** children get angry." However, the child may express anger light years beyond the anger of the normal child. Some kids are kids times ten!

🔑 *"So, learning rather than accomplishment is the issue of parenthood."*
Polly Berrien Berends

5. ONE YEAR FOR ONE YEAR

Some parents cling to the notion that for every year the adopted child was exposed to damaging conditions such as abuse, abandonment, and neglect, that it will take an equal amount of time to undo that damage. For example, if the child lived with abuse for the first three years of his life, then was removed from damage at that time, he should be normal by age six. Unfortunately, with some children the early injuries will affect their lives for years to come.

6. YOU NEED TO HANDLE YOUR OWN PROBLEMS

Rugged individualism is an all-American trait. Independence, freedom of thought, and a touch of daring–all contribute to the myth that as parents you need to handle all your own problems. This myth may lead to minor snafus when raising normal children, but it can be catastrophic in raising special needs youngsters. Sadly, all too many good adoptive parents distance themselves from others and set about parenting in isolation.

7. ADOPTION FINALIZATION WILL CHANGE THE CHILD FOR THE BETTER

Oh, if it were only true! If only legal finalization of adoption brought finality to the horrific history, meddlesome habits,

"Success consists of a series of little daily victories." Laddie F. Hutar

and chronic unhappiness of troubled children. Unfortunately, finalization is not the end. In actuality, finalization is a start, the trailhead of the life-long journey for the child and his adoptive family.

8. WE CAN CHANGE (READ: CURE) ALL KIDS

Pride goeth before the fall, and this myth precedes a close encounter with humility! Contrary to what we might suspect, some children will actually thwart the help, change, and improvement that foster families have to offer. Tragically, others may have suffered injuries which cannot be totally remediated. For this reason many families must examine their goals for troubled youngsters. One realistic adoptive parent vocalized, "If I can keep him out of the cemetery, correctional facilities, and chemical dependency until the age of 18 or so, I'll be very pleased!" Now, it may not be *that* extreme with most adoptive families; but, the point is that we need to temper optimism with realism.

QUESTIONS TO PONDER OR DISCUSS ☞

1. Which myth(s) do you now believe or have you believed in the past?

2. Do you expect that you will need assistance in your parenting?

3. When did you first realize that your expectations for your child were off target?

NOTES ✂ NOTES ✂ NOTES ✂ NOTES

NOTES ✒ NOTES ✒ NOTES ✒ NOTES

*It is important to remember that when it comes to advice,
it is easier to give than to receive.*

CHAPTER FOUR

Specific Advice-Giving

Note: Adopting a special needs child raises beaucoup questions in the minds of new parents: Why do kids do what they do? What should we expect next? Will these kids ever respond favorably to us? Are we the people for this job? While some parents may simply want to be told exactly what to do, most want a sounding board, a reality check, someone to bounce ideas off of. In this chapter we discuss the specifics of advice-giving, one of the central aspects of mentoring.

advice n. Somebody's opinion about what another person should do.

A doptive parents have questions, especially during crisis times, about whether they are doing what is right for their child. Hopefully during moments of urgency and emergency, they will reach out to each other for answers to these questions.

It reminds me of the story of the man who was learning to parachute. On his first jump, he counted to three and pulled the rip cord. Nothing happened. He calmed himself and pulled the cord for the back-up chute. Nothing again. By then he was falling earthward at a hundred miles an hour. Just then, a man streaked by him the other direction—going straight up at 100 mph. As they shot by each other, the parachutist yelled out, "Do you know anything about para-

45

chutes?" "No," the skyward man screamed back. "Do you know anything about propane?"

When a family is in free fall or when there is an explosive situation, it's nice to have someone to turn to with questions. Hopefully, mentors will have more to offer our new families than the unfortunate men in the story above.

A LITTLE ADVICE ABOUT GIVING ADVICE:

How and when to give advice to others is more art than science. Most of us have given advice to our children, our parents, or our colleagues. At times we are glad we offered our words of wisdom; at other times we wished we had kept our thoughts to ourselves. Our advice has been given when it was solicited, invited, or even demanded, "Tell me what I should do!" Occasionally, we have overstepped our bounds and advised others when they hadn't wanted it, sought it, or later appreciated or heeded it.

Whether solicited or unsolicited, once given, our counsel has undoubtedly resulted in a variety of responses. Sometimes advice is taken, sometimes rejected. Sometimes it is misunderstood, misinterpreted, or misapplied. Invariably we wonder if our advice was good or bad. Helpful or harmful. Conversely, if we hold our tongue or button our lip, we later ponder how things might have worked out if we had shared our perceptions, warnings, suggestions--that bit of free advice.

"The only good thing about free advice is its price."

It is important to remember that when it comes to advice, it is usually easier to give than to receive. Before offering advice, we should know our advisees. Do they seek advice? Do they need advice? Are they ready for advice?

Before offering advice, we should recall that our consultation should not replace or overshadow the task of compassionate listening. WE are not the problem-solvers. Though we want our experienced families to impart wisdom when needed and requested, mentor families should studiously avoid the tendency to tell others how they should parent.

A few caveats: advice-giving should avoid criticism, yet provide feedback; avoid pontification, yet offer alternative opinions; avoid dictating, yet provide encouraging suggestions. Very importantly, advice-giving should not settle for the quick solution at the expense of talking things out.

In many cases advice-giving can be inadvisable.

listen v. 1. To concentrate on hearing somebody or something. 2. To pay attention to something and take it into account.

wisdom n. The knowledge and experience needed to make sensible decisions and judgments.

Common Issues to Address with Advice:

We can give people advice about which stocks and bonds to invest in, how to save their marriage, and what house plants to buy. But, those issues are not at the crux of mentoring foster and adoptive parents. Mentoring advice will usually focus on aspects of parenting the troubled child, such as:

1. Controlling the urge to normalize,
2. Helping to set realistic expectations,

3. Engendering hope,

4. Dispelling parental guilt feelings,

5. Dealing with system-generated issues,

6. Rehearsing predictable crises, and

7. Innovative parenting.

Next, we will discuss advice-giving related to those seven aspects of parenting.

1. CONTROLLING THE URGE TO NORMALIZE:

normalize v. To make something or somebody conform to a standard.

Parents naturally look to normalize their children. When the baby is born, they inspect, scrutinize, count fingers and toes. Is my baby normal? They keep close watch on the milestones: when did he first smile, crawl, walk, and talk? Is he developing normally? When the child goes off to kindergarten, they make sure the child has the shoes on the right feet, obeys the teacher, and learns his first lessons. Is he learning correctly, fitting in normally?

When parents adopt, they also inspect, scrutinize, and keep close watch. And, if they have adopted a special needs child, they discover that there are things that are not normal. "Look how small and underfed he is!" "See how far behind he is academically!" "Watch how out of control his temper gets!" "See how immature he is emotionally!" "See how backward he is socially!"

Detecting the abnormalities, parents predictably try to do

something about it. They have the urge to help, to set things right, to catch the child up, and in general to "normalize" their child. Unfortunately, if the urge to help is too urgent, this in itself may produce problems. The child may perceive efforts to change him as a statement that he is not O.K. In the end, an urgency to normalize can result in:

•increased power struggles;
•suppression of the child's anger;
•resistance to attachments;
•clinging to abnormality.

Mentors can help new adopting parents by identifying any over-zealous urge to normalize.

2. HELPING TO SET REALISTIC GOALS AND EXPECTATIONS:

One of the most important areas of advice-giving centers on helping the mentee family to adopt realistic goals and expectations for their child. Most parents have conscious or unconscious aspirations for their child. Some of the aspirations are too high, some too low. When what the child attains and what the parent helps him attain fall short of the level of aspiration, it can be deflating and demoralizing for both. Setting aspirations at a level which can frequently find attainment engenders satisfactions which bolster parents and child alike. Here are some issues which often need to be addressed with mentees:

"A pint can't hold a quart–if it holds a pint it is doing all that can be expected of it."
Margaretta W. Deland

49

•some children may never be completely normal;
•some perceived behavior problems may actually be normal actions of children at that age;
•some academic problems should be addressed only by the school or by tutors;
•children's inherited disposition and early history of maltreatment can render them high risk for abnormalities.

Mentoring must help new foster and adoptive parents to scale back, calibrate, and/or re-think the goals they set for the child and themselves. Setting goals at the right level offers the opportunity for learning and growth. The goals must not be so lofty that they demoralize nor so low that they produce lassitude.

hope v. To have a wish to get or do something or for something to happen or be true, especially something that seems possible or likely.

3. ENGENDERING HOPE:

While no one has a crystal ball, we'd all like one. Especially with troubled youngsters, we would like to peer into the future. Will they make it? Will they ever straighten out? Will our efforts change their lives for the better?

"Aerodynamically, the bumblebee shouldn't be able to fly, but the bumblebee doesn't know it, so it goes on flying anyway."
Mary Kay Ash

One crucial area of advice-giving by mentors is that of counseling the mentees about hope. Without hope our efforts as parents may wither and vanish. Mentors may know of happy endings, or at least of outcomes which were more positive than negative about children who, without devoted families, would have been totally lost; and, who with good homes, found their way. Mentors can share hope-engendering advice in the following ways:

- •by sharing their own war stories about challenges they survived with kids;
- •by recounting how some children with difficult early problems eventually turned their lives around;
- •by revealing that ups and downs are predictable, inevitable;
- •by reassuring the parents that the overall trajectory of the child's life may be going up, even though there are dips along the way.

4. Dispelling Parental Guilt Feelings:

A comedian once said that guilt is the gift that keeps on giving. As we all know, good parents can usually find things to feel guilty about. Where did we go wrong? Was it that time that we accidentally dropped Johnny on his head?

One of the most predictable areas of guilt concerns the lack of feeling love for the child. Why don't I love this unfortunate child? Why do others love this child, yet I can't? Why does this child make me feel revulsion? What kind of a mother does not love her child?

Much of the mentor's focus may be on dispelling or relieving guilt feelings and on reducing pressures which guilt produces in parents. We must love this child—now!

Mentors may also address the guilt that parents feel about their anger toward the child. When mentees find out from

"This is one of the miracles of love: it gives a power of seeing through its own enchantments and yet not being disenchanted."
C. S. Lewis

guilt n. Self-reproach, causing feelings of shame and regret, for a wrongdoing or an inadequacy.

mentors that they too have felt anger toward their children, it can lift a burden which has discouraged and isolated the parents. It is crucial for mentors and mentees to frankly communicate about the soul-searching that parents engage in concerning their own welling anger. Too many adoptive parents raise the self-depreciating question, "What kind of parent can be angry at a child who has already been the butt of so much rage and abuse in his past?"

5. DEALING WITH SYSTEM-GENERATED ISSUES:

Some of the largest barriers to successful adoption are system issues. The adoptive families are not only beset by problems within the home; they also contend with macro system problems which can frustrate and deplete them.

In school, their children may have problem behaviors. The parents may be asked to remove or to homeschool their child. Though they are told of a homeschool partnership, they find that the school is a better talker than listener. It may advise the parents on how to handle the child at home, but may not listen to the parents about how the child should be handled at school.

In the mental health center, they may meet counselors who lack experience with troubled adopted youngsters. At the public welfare adoption unit, they find paltry support in terms of respite and other post-adoptive services.

In the community, the parents may go from saint to sinner very quickly. They are seen as the source of the child's problems. The underlying question is "Why haven't you gotten control of his behavior problems in our neighborhood?"

Mentors may have to be advance men, advocates, and champions for the mentees while they impart advice about how to handle these macrosystem issues. Mentors can provide support by:

- securing respite services;
- advocating for post adoption services, including fair subsidies;
- accompanying the mentees at school staffings;
- walking the mentees through the correctional and court system.

6. DRESS REHEARSALS FOR PREDICTABLE CRISES:

dress rehearsal n. A fullscale practice before any important event.

Sometimes advice-giving should focus on proactivity, that is on rehearsal, preparation, and advanced warning. Mentors can save mentees a lot of grief and heartache by looking ahead. Specifically, mentors may address the following in their advice-giving:

- what to expect with sexual abuse victims;
- which therapists are helpful;
- how to take care of one's marriage ahead of time;
- how children may split parents;

Mentors do not always pull a rabbit out of the hat, e.g. come up with perfect advice which fixes the child, straightens out the family, and generally astounds onlookers.

•grieving the loss of the life you used to have;
•maximizing the healing power of the other children in the home;
•permission to take respite;
•safeguarding the health of the original nuclear family;
•looking beyond surface behaviors to what they are really telling us;
•helping parents to avoid personalizing too much.

There can be great value in forewarning. Mentors who alert the parents about common problems that can pop up are offering prognostication, not pessimism.

7. INNOVATIVE PARENTING:

Most parents have been exposed to "good enough" parenting, e.g. the kind of parenting that works with the average situations which come up. Few adoptive parents, however, have knowledge of the kind of parenting it takes to reach truly disturbed children. There is the story about the adoptive parents who had newly placed twin boys, one who was a fire-setter and the other a bed-wetter. The mentor of this new family asked them to consider bunk beds. She called it a "trickle down" approach to the problem.

Mentors need to advise mentees on the advisability of remaining creative, analytic, and flexible in their parenting of difficult children. Introducing the use of parenting approaches such as "creating role familiarity," "keeping a clinical distance," etc. (see ahead) may be invaluable in staving

creative adj. Making imaginative use of the limited resources available.

analytic adj. Able or inclined to separate things into their constituent elements in order to study or examine them, draw conclusions, or solve problems.

flexible adj. Responsive to change according to circumstances; adaptable.

55

off mounting problems and getting parents unstuck with the child.

Lastly, it is important for advice-giving mentors to simply interact with and value the mentees. Sometimes we think of ourselves only as parents, or worse yet, as failing parents. Thus, it is essential for mentors to acknowledge the worth of the mentees as human beings who also happen to be parenting a tough kid or two. Beyond their successes and failures with the child, they are good and humane.

FINAL COMMENTS ABOUT ADVICE-GIVING

Here is some advice about advice-giving:

- Self-disclosure by mentors is okay in moderation.
- Sometimes it is not the advice but the mere presence of an advice-giver which offers the most.

In the words of mentors, Norm and Bonnie, many new families benefit when they experience mentors as "concerned witnesses to their struggle."

QUESTIONS TO PONDER OR DISCUSS ⚿

1. Do you seek specific advice? Would you prefer emotional support?

2. To whom do you currently turn for advice regarding your children and their problems?

3. Do you envision yourself as a mentor or mentee at present?

NOTES ⚭ NOTES ⚭ NOTES ⚭ NOTES

MENTORING THROUGH ADOPTION DISRUPTION

Note: This chapter focuses upon perhaps the saddest task in mentoring, e.g. helping other parents consider disruption.

None of us relish addressing the topic of adoption disruption or dissolution. Yet, termination of adoption is a fact of life, a tragic reality. (Related to this is the whole gamut of decisions to place the child outside the home for treatment, respite care, crisis care, and psychiatric hospital care. In such instances the child might never return home to live with the parents, though they retain legal custody. Technically, this would not be a dissolution or disruption.) Disruption and dissolution rates in special needs adoptions have been reported at 10%. However, these rates can be much higher depending on the age of the child at the time of adoption, e.g. older children with special needs are at greater risk of failing in placement. With our national emphasis on doubling the numbers of special needs adoptions, increases in adoptive disruptions will likely appear.

Following are several topics related to mentoring through the challenges of disruption:

⚷ Parenthood teaches you that there is more than one answer to every question in life.

59

•Broaching the subject of adoption disruption or dissolution;

•Talking with adoptive families who refuse to give up even though they must;

•Reassuring parents about what they have given to the child who must go;

•Dealing with grief issues in losing the child;

•Partial disruptions in a sibling group;

•Dealing with the "blame game." Going from saint to sinner in the eyes of your extended family, friends, community and "the system."

BROACHING THE SUBJECT OF ADOPTION DISRUPTION/DISSOLUTION:

"Silence is not always tact and it is tact that is golden, not silence."
Samual Butler

Unfortunately, some adoptions fizzle, flounder and fail. Some before legal finalization (disruption) and some after finalization (dissolution). Occasionally, the reasons for the dissolution/disruption are obvious and simple. More commonly, the causes of the demise are more hidden and/or more complicated. Mismatches, extreme behavior problems, attachment issues, sabotage, lack of support, may all play a part. In any case, the decision to end the adoption is rarely easy. More typically, it is wrenching and sometimes requires help from others. In some instances, others must broach the subject or encourage consideration of disruption or dissolution.

Some adoptive parents with stolid perseverance or guilty doggedness, struggle to make an adoption work, even though it may seriously impact their physical/mental health, other children in the home, etc. Some feel pressured to hang in there too long with the child(ren) due to well-intentioned but erroneous advice from relatives, friends, and helping professionals.

In the midst of the pressure, guilt, and vacillation, a decision must be made—but how, when and what? When is the time to seriously question the continuation of the adoption? How do we determine whether the adoption is terminally wounded, and what should specifically be decided about ending the adoption?

Mentors can be extremely helpful in providing support and advice to mentees through this ofttimes lonely, agonizing process. They may be the ones to introduce the hush-hush topic. The mentors often have a more objective, circumspect view of the fact that the adoption must end, or that the child may need to be moved. With superior clarity, mentors can see what holding onto the adoption is doing to the mentees. Additionally, they can observe when the point of diminishing returns becomes the point of no return.

WHEN FAMILIES REFUSE TO GIVE UP EVEN THOUGH THEY MUST:

🔑 *"The beginning of wisdom is to call things by their right name."* Chinese Proverb

Many adoptions have failed long before the adoptive parents know it or are willing to admit it. The parents' sense of commitment, obligation, and loyalty to the adopted child(ren) keeps them hanging on, even when objectively there is no hope left. Living with the hurt close-up, day-after-day, they often are unaware of how painful their lives have become.

Sometimes adoptive parents feel an undying devotion and a one-sided love toward the child which the child does not reciprocate. At other times, the husband may have more positive feelings about the child and may be experiencing acute pain in letting go of a child who has a more normal relationship to him than to his wife.

Whatever the case may be, the adoptive parents are often stymied; unable to decide whether or when to give up and cut the losses to themselves and the child. There are no clear guidelines to identify the terminal adoption, e.g. the adoption that cannot survive.

Mentors may be the first to recognize the signs of impending disruption/dissolution. They may observe that the mentee parents are refusing to give up, though the writing on the wall is in capital letters. Mentors can point out the increasingly obvious and gently confront the refusal to consider the compelling signs of impending dissolution/disruption.

REASSURING PARENTS ABOUT WHAT THEY HAVE GIVEN TO THE CHILD:

When an adoption is failing or has failed, adoptive parents need reassurance. They ask themselves many soul-searching questions: Are we giving up too early on this child? Have we hurt the child more than helped him? Will our dissolution of the adoption damage the child irreparably? Have we sought out all the help that we or the child needed? What does ending the adoption say about us as parents? Why can't we love this child? Are we total failures?

All of these questions (and more) haunt the parents. Mentors need to provide understanding and compassion as well as reassurance to the mentees about the gifts they have given to the child. The child may not have accepted the gifts, but the mentors need to acknowledge and affirm that the mentors have tried. It is equally important for mentors to point out that the positive effects of the mentees' gifts to the child may only be realized in the future.

Further, it is vital for mentors to convey that some children are unreachable by any family. Each special needs'placement holds the inherent risk that the adoption may dissolve or disrupt. Lastly, it is crucial for mentors to underscore that no parent can reach every child. Even our most experienced, highly trained treatment foster parents can meet their Waterloo with a specific troubled child.

"The garden loves the rain and, yes, this is love. But the love I want for you– the love I want to give you–is the love the rain gives the garden. Loving is giving freedom."
Peter McWilliams

63

DEALING WITH GRIEF ISSUES IN LOSING THE CHILD:

When adoptions end, loss is everywhere. With loss comes grief. The adoptive family mourns the loss of the child, the loss of a dream, and sometimes a loss of self-esteem. The child loses a home, a family, and a potential shot at permanence. In the aftermath, the child is often provided counseling or psychotherapy to deal with that loss, to help him grieve. But, it is rare for the family to receive comparable assistance.

I believe that we owe post-disruption support to any family who relinquishes a placement. Without it they may find their marriage in trouble, their health suffering, their parenting of other remaining children degraded. (This also happens to many foster parents whose cumulative loss of children goes unaided until their charitable parenting instincts expire.)

Mentors can provide a valuable function to grieving adopters by recognizing the need to grieve and by endorsing the grief, frustration, and disappointment which the family feels.

I dare say that sometimes the adopters experience more loss and a stronger grief reaction than the adopted child. This is especially true in situations where the child has resisted attachment, while the adopters developed a unilateral, unrequited bond.

🔑 *"and through all the tears and the sadness and the pain comes the one thought that can make me internally smile again: I have loved."*
Peter McWilliams

PARTIAL DISRUPTIONS IN SIBLING GROUPS:

The past decade has seen an upsurge in placement of sibling groups. The sometimes laudatory practice of placing brothers and sisters jointly may occasionally result in disruption, at least of one of the children. In some unfortunate cases, the collective pathology of a sibling group may overburden the adoptive parents and precipitate a disruption. In other instances, while one or more siblings with lesser pathology do well, the individual pathology in one child may thwart successful incorporation of the whole into the adoptive home.

"Life is playing a violin solo in public and learning the instrument as one goes on."
Samuel Butler

When disruptions involving siblings occur, special issues arise:
- How to communicate to the children about the disruption? (e.g. the child who is going and the child who is staying.)
- How to allay the anxieties of the child who stays but fears he may be the next to go.
- Dealing with judgmental outsiders.
- Setting up proper on-going contact between siblings after the disruption.
- Coping with any implied threats from workers or agencies to remove the other children.

THE BLAME GAME:

In the case of dissolution/disruption, blaming is rampant. It's ubiquitous but comes from two usual directions: e.g. from without, therapists, caseworkers, neighbors, relatives and friends contribute. From within, the harsh voice of conscience and the most plaguing of parental questions. What did we do wrong?

"False guilt is guilt felt at not being what other people feel one ought to be or assume that one is."
R.D. Laing,
The Self and Others

There is a natural tendency to blame adopters who disrupt. Harsh judgment of others is common. How can they give the poor child away? What will this rejection do to the child? What kind of parent gives up on his/her child? Has the family tried as hard as it could? Did the parents create the problem which they complain the child has?

These questions parallel and reinforce the internal doubts and questions of the adopters. Could we have done more? What kind of people are we anyway? Did we harm the child more than help him? Are we simply bad parents? And, of course, one of the hardest questions: should we feel guilty about feeling so relieved that the child is gone from our home?

Mentors can bring balance, reason and the assurance that parents do not need to accept undeserved blame. It is healthier to grieve than to self-blame.

An unfortunate quirk in child abuse statutes in many states is that if the adoptive parents attempt to give back an adopted child, they must be, in the eyes of the system, abusers. Adoptive parents find themselves declared neglecting parents. Often a "D and N" proceeding must determine that the child is de facto dependent, neglected and/or beyond the control of his adoptive parents. This declaration adds insult to injury since the family, already feeling like miserable failures, now has the official judgment of the courts, which confirms their status as bad parents.

FINAL COMMENTS:

Whenever we neglect adoptive parents during dissolution or disruption, we do an inexcusable disservice. At the time of disruption, these families feel the most isolated, despondent, and directionless. They also feel punished and judged. In hindsight, they reflect, "Maybe we were not intended to adopt children. Maybe we are unfit for any adopted child."

To allow adoptive parents to remain estranged fuels an unjustified self-punishment. It leaves the parents feeling they had no business adopting. Left with that often erroneous conclusion, they may become a lost resource to other children in the future.

"It is a risk to love. What if it doesn't work out? Ah, but what if it does?"
Peter McWilliams

QUESTIONS TO PONDER OR DISCUSS ⚡

CHAPTER FIVE

1. Has the thought of disruption ever occurred to you?

2. Do you know other parents who have ended an adoption?

3. Have you ever needed to place an adopted child outside your home (e.g. a hospital, a Residential Treatment Center, a shelter home)?

NOTES ⚮ NOTES ⚮ NOTES ⚮ NOTES

NOTES ⚮ NOTES ⚮ NOTES ⚮ NOTES

CHAPTER SIX

MENTORING REGARDING STRATEGIES

Note: This chapter addresses the importance of sharing parental strategies. Specifically, the mentor and mentee may need to discuss specific parenting approaches with emphasis on the needs of the child, the history the child has experienced, and the mentee's family values.

"There are only two ways of meeting difficulties. You alter the difficulties or you alter yourself to meet them."
Phyliss Bottome

Most first-time, adoptive parents assume that the parenting they grew up with or the parenting they used with their birth children will suffice with troubled adopted kids. However, sometimes they are very wrong. When these parents discover that typical parenting is not working with the child, hopefully, they turn to others for ideas. That's when the mentors can be crucial. Helping develop alternative ways of looking at behavior problems and intervention is an essential mentor task.

In this chapter we will introduce notions related to atypical parenting approaches which might help. We will look at several issues:

•How to identify and deal with a child who is used to taking care of himself alone and rebuffs efforts from adults to parent him.

•How to determine what roles the child has histori-

71

cally assumed and when it may be advisable to allow the child to play out or assume that role again.

•How to encourage parents to stand back, to analyze, and to not take the child's behavior personally.

•How to clarify their understanding of the child's beliefs and hidden expectations.

•How to ease up on the pressure to attach to the child quickly.

•How to decipher the child's encrypted messages and interpret behavioral language.

•How to contain the child's unhealthy tendency to split adults.

1. Building a Bridge to the Island.

Many troubled foster and adopted children gave up on parent figures long ago. Could they count on parents? No. Could they get what they needed from parents? Never. Could they expect the parent to be physically present, let alone emotionally available? Not likely.

CASE STUDY: *Billy refused to eat at the dinner table with his adoptive family. He'd piddle with his food, but he avoided eating. The adoptive parents were concerned about this and about*

⚷ *"The second principle of magic: ...things which have once been in contact with each other continue to act on each other at a distance after the physical contact has been severed."*
Sir James G. Frazer

the related fact that Billy was raiding the refrigerator after hours. While they were thankful that he was eating something and not starving himself, they felt Billy was symbolically refusing to join the family. An experienced foster parent who had befriended the adoptive parents, suggested that Billy might be refusing to swallow what the family had to offer in more ways than at the dinner table.

In her own assessment of Billy, the adoptive mother remarked: "Whoever said, 'No man is an island' didn't know this child."

DISCUSSION: Given what they have been through with parents, troubled foster and adopted children like Billy assume that no one will be concerned about their needs. Thus, they grow to believe that their needs cannot be met within a parent-child relationship. They have learned to look out for themselves. Oftentimes, this leads to secretive, solitary, underground modes of addressing needs. The child becomes an island. And correspondingly, foster or adoptive parents of this child feel banished from the island.

When children lead an insular lifestyle, one which excludes parents, we must find a bridge. Otherwise the child effectively prevents new learning, corrective experiences, and encounters with parent figures which might alter his assumptions.

INTERVENTIONS: To address this on-going problem of stealing food, the mentors and mentees discussed leaving a bowl of food out for Billy, allowing him free access to food at all times. They also talked about taking Billy grocery shopping and allowing him to help in the selection of foods which he likes. (Giving him some sense of control over food selection might encourage him to join in other food related activities, specifically eating food with the family.) Additionally, the mentors suggested hand-feeding Billy as one might feed a baby. They discussed having Billy sit on the mother's lap and her spoon feeding him. Lastly, the mentor's suggested that if Billy enjoyed fooling the adult world by outsmarting them with his food stealing, the adoptive family might actually hide some of Billy's favorite foods around the house and make a game of it for him.

In each of the interventions discussed by the mentors and mentees, the emphasis was placed on putting parents into the child's insular world. This would allow Billy to experience caretakers as helping to supply his needs.

2. CREATING ROLE FAMILIARITY.

"Far more than techniques and practices that may have worked in other situations, you need an approach that will enable you, even empower you, to apply principles in your situation."
Stephen R. Covey

When a child moves into a new home, foster or adoptive, it can be a big shock. The child feels the shock of moving away from family, neighborhood, school/playmates, and/or cultural roots. Shocking, jolting, disorienting. And yes, the child may also experience one more shock: role shock. When the child moves into a foster or adoptive family, he may find that his historic role in past family life is already taken or nonexistant.

Troubled children may historically have played one or more of the following roles in previous dysfunctional family settings: marriage counselor, confidante, surrogate parent, paramedic, and/or sexual partner. The following case study focuses on a child who took on the parental role.

CASE STUDY: *Joleene was a ten-year-old go-getter. Hyperactive and parental, she was "take charge" with her two younger brothers. She was unrelenting in her bossiness and parental behaviors. Historically, she had always been the mother figure by default. Her birth mother was inert, passive and often incapacitated by a substance abuse problem. Once placed in the foster/adoptive family, the three children played out their old roles. Joleene clung tenaciously to the familiar role of "little mother," expanding it to include bossing the birth children of the adoptive parents. The adoptive parents found Joleene's maintenance of the parental role undermining of their authority. No amount of correction and explanation seemed to dissuade Joleene from her appointed tasks.*

DISCUSSION: When a child enters a foster or adoptive home, he/she often automatically adopts the role that is familiar. However, the child may find herself vying for a role which is already taken. Her assumption of the role is unneeded, unwanted and/or rejected outright by the new family. The adoptive mother and father may have a good marriage, negating the need for the child to attempt to save the marriage, to reduce conflict, to distract with her own problems, etc. The mother may be an independent, competent individual who has adult friends, a good marriage, and extended family with whom she communicates and in whom she confides. Since the adoptive mother fulfills her role adequately, the family does not have an opening for another mother figure. Other children in the home already look to this mother for direction, comfort, and safety. Additionally, the child is not needed to minister to the medical or psychiatric needs of an adult, since the foster or adoptive parents are physically and emotionally healthy. If there is a problem, they do not expect the child to handle it. Lastly, the child is not coerced or invited into a sexual relationship with other family members. Sexual activity is confined to the marriage, or, in the case of a single parent, sexual intimacy is not sought from children. In any case, the child may feel extraordinarily out of sorts without her familiar role.

POSSIBLE INTERVENTION: In situations where a child stubbornly refuses to surrender an historic role, it may be best to employ "role familiarity." The adoptive family may need to resist the tendency to change the child quickly. They might consider allowing or even endorsing the best parts of the child's behavior. One experienced foster parent suggested to her mentee that she pay the child for the parental behavior she emitted. (e.g. Pay the child and praise her for what she often does automatically, reflexively.) Ironically, paying the child gives the child pause for thought. It draws attention to the child's behavior but without any negativity. The parent might say, "Thank you for listening to your sister. Here's a quarter." "Good girl, you are so nice to diaper your sister. Here's fifty cents."

After six to eight weeks of establishing this pay-for-parenting pattern, the parent abruptly ceases all payment. Once having been paid for a behavior, many children flatly refuse to act without remuneration. Thus, the parentified behavior tends to reduce or disappear.

3. KEEPING A CLINICAL DISTANCE.

It is not easy to stay objective while parenting difficult children. As parents, we can be swept up in the act of parenting. And, parenting reaches us at all levels: emotional, physical, intellectual, and spiritual. Robots don't raise children—yet.

As parents, it is easy to take the things our children say and do personally. Parenting is supposed to be personal, not impersonal. But, at times children elicit from us strong emotions which cloud our judgment, creativity, and sense of direction, as in the following case.

"When you are dealing with a child, keep all your wits about you, and sit on the floor."
Austin O'Malley

CASE STUDY: *When Lila, a single mother, was referred to me with an adoption in distress, I found that she had taken in a sibling group of three. She got along fine with the baby, an eighteen-month-old girl, who was already bonded to her after eight months of placement. The oldest of the three, an eight-year-old girl, was beginning to fit in. However, Lila encountered insurmountable problems with the middle child, Annie, a six-year-old girl. Annie had sustained mild brain injury at birth, which had rendered her hyperactive and seriously language delayed. It made her difficult—difficult to control, difficult to communicate with, difficult to understand, and very difficult to love or like.*

Lila felt she was in a hostage situation. The human services adoption unit had informed her that she could not give the middle child back to them separate from the siblings. It was a package, an all-or-nothing placement. Clearly, Lila loved two of the three children. But, she struggled with Annie, who seemed angry with her but would never articulate it. Annie used the "don't get mad, get vengeful" approach to handling any conflict in the adoptive home. Historically, she had been the child which the birth mother liked least. And, having been given very little warm attention from her birth mother, Annie had developed ways of securing attention, albeit negative attention.

DISCUSSION: Not surprisingly, Lila felt disturbed by the unearned anger she inherited from the unsatisfactory biological mother-daughter relationship. A forthright, outspoken woman, Lila was flummoxed by Annie's total lack of candor and refusal to communicate with emotional honesty. Lila felt like her frank parenting approach was thwarted by her daughter's penchant for indirectness. Not surprisingly, Lila took things quite personally; and she felt like a failure.

INTERVENTION: In cases like this, a parent may need to employ "clinical distance" to reach the child. Specifically, the adoptive mother might reduce her demand for candor from the child. An acceptance of imperfect candor might be her intermediate goal with her child. (When parents of troubled children expect impeccable candor or honesty, it is a set-up for exasperation.) Additionally, Lila may need to take things less to heart, step back, and without becoming aloof or withdrawn, remove herself as a vulnerable target.

The mentors suggested that Lila take a clinical posture - keep a clinical distance to focus on what Annie's behavior was telling her, and how that might relate to her history. This approach allowed Lila to gain perspective, to step back from the negativity, and to reduce the pressure she had placed upon herself to love Annie as much the other children.

Interestingly, when Lila later verbalized to Annie that her lying said "stay away," the child burst into tears. (Lila had not confronted or cross-examined Annie about her lack of candor.) Lila felt wonderful about her daughter's tears, because her words had made an impact. It was a starting point! The artificial, deceitful child she had experienced before repulsed her, especially given her preference for honesty in relationships.

4. Identifying And Labeling The Child's Beliefs.

Many troubled foster and adopted children have suffered through life experiences which have marked them indelibly. Aside from any physical injury, there are unmistakable, undeniable psychological hurts which profoundly affect the child, his security, his recollections, his expectations, and even his most fundamental, core beliefs.

Although the child has no written set of beliefs, his behavior grows out of an often unstated, sometimes subconscious credo. This credo may contain one or more of the following twelve beliefs:

"Success is failure turned inside out."
Anon

☞ "Childhood is frequently a solemn business for those inside it."
George F. Will

•Reveal yourself to no one, if you want real safety.

•Expecting fairness is out of the question.

•Revenge is justified, because I am a victim.

•Keep score of what you have been denied, not what you've been given.

•Adults and children are engaged in an undeclared war.

•It's better to get negative attention than none at all.

•The only truth is what can be proven or dis-proven.

•Take care of numero uno.

•A compliment from a parent is only another form of control.

•Feeling close emotionally only leads to major hurt.

•Trust nobody.

•Acting-out can get you what you want or where you want to be.

CASE STUDY: *Eleven-year-old Greta had not really "bought into" the adoption. Indeed, she acted out continuously by soiling herself, smearing her feces on the wall, and generally mak-*

ing herself a smelly, unattractive child. The adoptive parents suspected this was Greta's attempt at undermining the adoption and her way of "raising a stink" about being adopted. They divined that Greta ultimately desired to return to her birth mother.

DISCUSSION: When a child lives by any of the previously listed, twelve beliefs and yet does not verbalize or understand them, behavior problems follow. As with Greta's soiling, where her belief is "acting-out can get you what you want or where you want to be." Specifically, if she acts-out enough, she can sabotage the placement and perhaps move home to her birth mother.

INTERVENTIONS: The adoptive parents were encouraged by their mentor couple to label beliefs and feelings for Greta, which were heretofore acted-out but not articulated.

The adoptive mother verbalized on several occasions, "Greta, you believe that if you act badly enough and smell badly enough, that we won't want you and you will be sent back to live with your mother." These remarks seemed to register with Greta, who commented snidely, "It worked before!" (e.g. she was referring to a previous disruption in foster placement.) The acting-out continued, despite the accuracy of the adoptive mother's labeling. (Accurate labeling is no guarantee of improvement in a child's behavior. In some situations the basic belief must be more than labeled, it must be confronted and challenged with "reality therapy.")

"Misery is when grown-ups don't realize how miserable kids can feel."
Suzanne Heller

Taking the next step, the adoptive parents, caseworker, and birth mother met jointly with Greta to reiterate that the birth mother had no intention of taking Greta back. (Sadly, birth parents do not often support the adoptive effort. In those cases, involvement in such a joint meeting may be contra-indicated entirely.) After this reality check, Greta appeared to reduce her sabotaging behavior, at least for several weeks.

5. REDUCING THE PRESSURE TO ATTACH.

Although we might be loath to admit it, there is often an un-fair pressure placed on both the child and the adoptive par-ent to attach on cue. That is, once the placement is com-pleted or the adoption finalized, the race is on. The child should be attaching to the parent, and the parent should be feeling a growing bond to the child. It is as if there were some hidden time schedule. By the end of the first month, a par-ent should feel 75% attached while the child should feel somewhere between 25% and 50% of normal expectable attachment. By the end of the first trimester of placement, the parent should not detect any appreciable difference in loving bonds to the adoptive child compared with birth chil-dren, and so on. Sometimes this pressure on adoptive par-ents to attach poste haste is self-inflicted.

CASE STUDY: *Brandon, age 14, had suffered three failed adop-tions and countless foster home placements. A master sabo-teur, he had undermined the adoptive placements due to "at-tachment phobia." Finally placed in a group home permanently, he was informed that he would not be adopted by the group home parents. Ironically, Brandon grew extremely attached to the group home parents and remained in their home through high school graduation.*

DISCUSSION: Many adoptive parents are familiar with children who are attachment phobic like Brandon. Given their ultra-sensitivity to growing attachment, these youngsters may require special treatment. Specifically, the adoptive parents may want to dramatically de-emphasize any pressures on the child to attach or commit. Any sense of urgency must go. Once the child senses urgency, e.g. the demand for intimacy, he may resist fanatically.

The parent, painfully aware of the relationship vacuum, often feels inadequate, guilty and angry with herself or the child. What kind of parent feels dead inside toward a needy child? Dare I reveal to anyone that I still feel nothing for this child after six months?

INTERVENTION: One adoptive family created the so-called "backhanded compliment" strategy with an adopted daughter who would backslide any time mention was made about how close family members felt toward her. The backhanded compliment involved offering a compliment and then simultaneously, ostensibly, taking it back. For example, the adoptive mother would say, "I'd like to mention how proud I've been of you lately, but I think I better not bring it up because it would upset you." With these so-called backhanded compliments, the adoptive mother hoped to make her positive

"You must have long range goals to keep you from being frustrated by short range failures." George H. Bender

83

sentiments palatable to her child.

6. TRANSLATING BEHAVIOR INTO WORDS, OR, PROBLEM BEHAVIOR IS LANGUAGE.

With some children we find ourselves acting more like cipher experts, ferreting out the meaning of words, deciphering hidden messages, cracking a code which comes in the form of baffling behavior problems. Frequently, all we have are partial clues, an unclear history, and/or notes concerning past placements. Many adopted youngsters don't have the foggiest idea what drives them. If they do, they may feel unwilling to say it out loud. So, we play Sherlock Holmes.

CASE STUDY: *Michelle was a ten-year-old girl with much to be angry about. She had been sexually abused earlier in her life by a stepfather. Intimidated by this man, she had developed hidden expressions for her anger at home. At school, she raged at the teachers and assaulted other children.*

When finally placed in foster care, Michelle carried over her school rages into the family setting. The foster parents were greatly taken aback by Michelle's temper outbursts, which they censured with verbal confrontation, especially from the foster father. Michelle, unable to distinguish present verbal confrontation from past verbal abuse, felt intimidated by the foster father. Almost immediately, she gained control over her anger outbursts, but simultaneously (it was later deduced) began wetting and hiding her underwear. At that point, she became totally mum in the feelings department.

DISCUSSION: In some cases children may have entered the foster or adoptive home quite loudly. They might show anger quite publicly and, for lack of a better word, crudely - yelling, screaming, tantrums, etc. Typically this does not go over very well with the foster or adoptive parents. Accordingly, the tendency is to curb or squelch this behavior, sometimes ill-advisedly. Clamping down on the outward manifestations of anger may eliminate the surface behavior but pushes the problem underground. Subsequently, the child often expresses strong feelings in sneaky, indirect and baffling ways, as in Michelle's case.

While it is normal for parents to dislike tantrums, it is not always prudent to contain the primitive outward expression of anger. How parents deal with the child's anger can move things forward or backward. If they can shape crude expressions gradually toward acceptable verbalizations, the child benefits. However, if the parents abruptly quash the behavior, the child may regress, conceal and submerge emotion. As a result, parenting is riddled with guesswork.

INTERVENTION: For Michelle to gain control of her current problem with wetting and hiding underwear, she will have to articulate her anger. The adoptive parents need to find acceptable ways for her to vent anger verbally. Indeed, they may need to invite, coach, and even press Michelle to say what she is mad about. The anger behind her symptoms must find expression in words.

"The way you treat any relationship in the family will eventually affect every relationship in the family."
Stephen R. Covey

7. THERAPEUTIC SPLITTING.

Many disturbed children become masterful "splitters." That is, they learn to fragment, partition, and divide-and-conquer their caretakers. In doing so, they often cause a great deal of mayhem by pitting one adult against the other. With adults in disharmony around them, these troubled children can maintain an unhealthy status quo while their dysfunctional interactions with others remain unchanged.

Often adopted youngsters idealize teachers, caseworkers, therapists, neighbors, birth parents or siblings, while devaluing their adoptive mothers and fathers. Not surprisingly, the idealized relationships fail to offer what a real and healthy attachment could. The tendency to simplistically divide individuals into "all good" or "all bad" categories prevents the formation of real attachments to real people.

CASE STUDY: *Fredrico, 17, and his older brother, Donald, 20, were adopted at the ages of five and eight by the Martino family. These brothers were street children for two years after being abandoned by their birth parents. They had witnessed much domestic violence prior to the abandonment and were chronically neglected as well. Once they were finally rounded up by the authorities, they were placed briefly in a receiving home and subsequently with the Martino family for adoption.*

In the adoptive family, Donald at first persisted in, then ultimately discontinued his historic protector role toward Fredrico. In response to the shift in their relationship, Fredrico became angry and demanding toward Donald while staunchly reject-

ing Mr. and Mrs. Martino. Fredrico, not so secretly, continued to pine for the inordinately close relationship to Donald. None- theless, Donald completely discarded his past parental role. Fredrico took this as personal rejection. Feelings of abandon- ment and bitterness mounted.

Over ten years' time, the relationship between the boys became almost exclusively rancorous. When Donald moved away at age 18, Fredrico shifted his anger to the Martinos. He shut them out emotionally and grew constantly moody and emotionally un- stable. At the same time he refused counseling and prescribed medication (e.g. antidepressants). Donald experienced minor trouble with the law: violating curfew, shoplifting and drinking. When his parents came to bail him out of jail, he cursed them and immediately ran away from home. At that time he falsely alleged that his parents were physically abusing him. He obvi- ously viewed the Martinos as the enemy, and his acting-out be- havior communicated his desire to distance them.

DISCUSSION: From day one Fredrico consistently refused to be part of the Martino family. Over the years, he feared father figures and viewed mother figures as abandoning. He spent years rebuffing the adoptive parents, while he sought closeness from a brother who was no longer parental.

When Donald ultimately left home, Fredrico never grieved the loss. Instead, the negative intensity of the relationship to his adoptive parents increased dramatically. Acting-out en- sued. When placed briefly at a local teen crisis shelter, Fredrico played the victim, provoking other youth to bully him. Addi- tionally, he appeared quite comfortable in the shelter, professing that he did not want to go back home. The staff erroneously assumed this had something to do with Mr. and Mrs. Martino (e.g. why would a child not want to go back home unless he was being mistreated, neglected, etc.?).

Oddly enough, while Fredrico asserted that he wanted nothing to do with his adoptive parents, he called home each day to tell them that he did not want to talk or to return home! Staff observed that with on-going overtures and invitations from the adoptive parents to come back home, Fredrico persisted ever more strongly in resisting a return home. Likewise, he persevered in placing his adoptive parents in the "bad guy" role. Complicating things further, Fredrico refused the psychotropic medications which had helped his moods measurably. Overall, behavior in the teen crisis shelter (and much of his negative behavior in the home) pointed to extreme ambivalence about family life. That is, he simultaneously wants and does not want to belong (e.d. his daily call home).

INTERVENTION: Unable and/or unwilling to belong emotionally or to connect meaningfully, Fredrico hid from intimacy in the upheaval he had created. His penchant for splitting adults into camps and the resultant turmoil shielded Fredrico from closeness. As the Martinos pressed for him to join the fold, Fredrico automatically resisted. Indeed, he had become expert at rejecting the offer of love, belonging and family.

The intervention suggested by the mentoring family involved "therapeutic splitting." After Fredrico was placed a second

⚷ *"He drew a circle that shut me out–*
Heretic, rebel, a thing to flaunt.
But love and I had the wit to win;
We drew a circle and took him in."
Edward Markham

time in the teen crisis shelter, the Martinos were advised by their mentors to try a new approach and to radically change their typical role. More specifically, the parents were advised to studiously discontinue pressuring or inviting Fredrico to return home. In family therapy meetings at the shelter, the staff was to adopt the parents' former role. That is, program staff would send a strong message that Fredrico must go home and work on becoming a part of the Martino family. For their part, the parents would adopt an understanding but somewhat neutral role. They would remark, "Maybe he needs additional time. He does so well in the shelter home." Also, they would assert on his behalf, "But Fredrico has had such a tough life which has made it so painful to be part of our home." The rejoinder from staff would be, "Of course he does well here. This shelter is not a family. For his benefit he needs to belong to your family." Taking their new role a step further, the Martinos would counter, "But he is afraid to belong and to feel good about belonging, because his life has been so hard. We can understand why he fights it."

Overall in this "therapeutic split," we asked staff, therapists, and workers (e.g. non-family members) to embrace one side of Fredrico's ambivalence–the side of Fredrico which secretly wants to be part of a family. These individuals then act as the driving force which presses him to do that, while the parents identify with Fredrico's hesitation, fear and refusal. While they attest their love for him, the Martinos should simultaneously voice their reluctance to force themselves on him. That is, they neither slam the door in Fredrico's face, nor force him through the open door.

The hoped-for response in this case is for the reluctant, resistant youngster to take a step toward family living. With others outside the family (e.g. shelter staff) taking on a more forceful role, the youth can transfer angry feelings toward them. Having been assigned the "bad guy" role in this therapeutic split, the staff become the easy target for Fredrico's rejection. Assigned the role of understanding but neutral "good guy," the Martinos join with Fredrico and his hesitation, resistance, and fear. In the therapeutic split, this joining tends to neutralize or at least diminish the anger directed at the Martinos by Fredrico. With any luck, this strategy may permit the Martinos a new opening.

QUESTIONS TO PONDER OR DISCUSS 🔑

1. Have you ever run out of parenting ideas for your child?

2. To whom do you turn for parenting advice and suggestions?

3. Have you ever created any unusual interventions to help with your child?

NOTES ⚬ NOTES ⚬ NOTES ⚬ NOTES

NOTES ☞ NOTES ☞ NOTES ☞ NOTES

Confidentiality is an important topic for discussion.

CONFIDENTIALITY

Confidential is defined by Merriam-Webster's as "secret, private, hushed, chummy, intimate, and trustworthy." These adjectives describe an essential dimension of the mentoring relationship. Without an understanding about confidentiality and lacking confidence in the privacy of the meetings and discussions, parents would be reluctant to openly discuss feelings, questions and problems.

Thus, confidentiality is an important topic for discussion at the outset of establishing a mentoring relationship. Mentors and mentees must come to an explicit understanding and agreement about the importance and specifics of confidentiality. The agreement should include, at a minimum, the following points:

> 1. None of the parties will disclose personal information discussed in their meetings to others outside of the meetings, except with direct permission.
>
> 2. Information concerning the children discussed is private, unless otherwise specified.
>
> 3. In states where mentors are mandatory reporters of child abuse, the requirements and conditions of reporting will be disclosed before the start of mentoring.

"Loyalty is more valuable than diamonds."
Philippine Proverb

Afterword

"To know the road ahead, ask those coming back."
Chinese Proverb

Mentoring of adoptive (or foster) parents by seasoned veteran parents is a notion whose time has come. Of course, mentoring occurs day-in-day-out in informal ways for parents of all sorts. Grandmothers mentor their daughters and sons. Mothers-in-law impart their wisdom to daughters-in-law. And friends with kids talk to other friends with kids.

With adoptive (and foster) parents raising special needs kids, mentoring is not so readily available. Advice is plentiful. But, good advice is few and far between. Often, it takes a parent who has been there, done that, and can communicate to less experienced individuals in a manner that is helpful and palatable.

The mentoring program tested by "Parent 2 Parent" and promulgated throughout Montana is by no means the only way to offer mentoring supports to new parents. In some communities, standard adoptive and foster parent support groups already provide exemplary direction for their members. Increasingly, parents find mentoring via cyberspace, e.g. through chatrooms on the Internet. Parent support groups, standard or cyber, can certainly diminish isolation and disseminate information. We hope that the "Parent 2 Parent" program contributes to the ways that adoptive parents are supported.

As a final note, I am pleased to report that mentoring seems to be taking on a life of its own. That is, those mentees who have been successfully mentored have evolved into mentors for even newer adoptive parents. Notably, Chris and Glen have now begun to reach out to others who are just beginning their journey and are attempting to find "safe passage" for themselves and their adopted children.

"If we could sell our experiences for what they cost us we'd be millionaires."
Abigail Van Buren

NOTES ⚬ NOTES ⚬ NOTES ⚬ NOTES

APPENDICES

THE ATTACHMENT CONTINUUM

This figure illustrates the attachment continuum which can be used to pinpoint the quality of attachment of any foster or adoptive child. On the far left of the continuum falls "marginal attachment" which is characterized by a paranoid picture of reality, lack of conscience, exploitation of others, lack of empathy, lack of long-term friendships, tyrannical control of others, and a basic distrust of the world. Children (and adults) with these characteristics have frequently been described, sometimes accurately, as "unattached."

On the far right of the continuum falls "overly attached" which is characterized by a limited picture of reality, overactive conscience, overdependency upon others, an inability to distinguish own from others' feelings and opinions, inordinate need to affiliate, need to be controlled, and a basic insecurity. In some troubled adolescents, over attachment may be diagnosed as borderline personality disorder.

At the midpoint of the continuum lies "normally attached" which is characterized by an accurate picture of reality, well formed conscience, generosity, role-taking ability, loyalties, democratic interactions, and a basic trust about the world. Sadly, few troubled foster or adopted children fall at this point on the continuum.

THE ATTACHMENT CONTINUUM

1 2 3	4 5 6	7 8 9
MARGINALLY ATTACHED	NORMALLY ATTACHED	OVERLY ATTACHED

CHARACTERISTICS:

• Paranoid picture of reality	• Accurate picture of reality	• Limited picture of reality
• Lack of conscience	• Well-formed conscience	• Overactive conscience
• Exploitation of others	• Generosity	• Overdependency on others
• Lack of empathy	• Role-taking ability	• Inability to distinguish own feeling and opinions from others
• No long-term friendships	• Loyalties	• Inordinate need to affiliate
• Tyrannical control of others	• Democratic interaction	• Need to be controlled
• Basic distrust	• Basic trust	• Basic insecurity

POSSIBLE RELATED DIAGNOSIS:

SOCIOPATHIC/ UNATTACHED	NORMAL	BORDERLINE/ OVERANXIOUS

101

PARENT 2 PARENT
THE VIDEOTAPE

advocate n. Somebody who acts or intercedes on behalf of another.

The videotape, "Parent 2 Parent," was developed to illustrate many of the points discussed in this guidebook. In the video, Chris and Glen, the mentee couple, converse with Norm and Bonnie, the mentor couple. Dr. Rick Delaney moderates the conversation. Salient points covered during the tape include:

> The advocacy role of mentors;
> Practical advice-giving by mentors;
> Healthy venting of emotions;
> Rehearsing "predictable crises;"
> Emotional rewards for the mentors; and
> Engendering hope in new families.

The purpose of the video is to show a glimpse of the initial "test case" mentor and mentee couples–to put a face on the process of mentoring. The written word cannot convey the warmth, humor, chemistry, and teamwork of the mentoring notion as well as the video snippets can. Despite the limitations of the printed page, here are a few comments about the points raised in the video:

1. THE ADVOCACY ROLE OF MENTORS

A central role of mentors is that of advocate, one who speaks on behalf of another. Early in the video, Chris underlines the importance of Norm and Bonnie as her "gallery of support," a reinforcement that she was okay. When their children's disturbing problems were observed and the local community passed judgment on the parents, the mentors were spokespersons, advocates, and defenders against detractors. More positively, the mentors worked to rally community support for the family. (Such support can falter when children's emotional and behavioral problems spill over into the school, neighborhood, and larger community.) Chris' comments underscore the importance of advocacy. The association with the mentor couple provides added credibility to the hard work done by the adoptive family. Truly, Norm and Bonnie played the advocate role, taking up the cause for Chris and Glenn.

"You take something out of your mind, garnished in kindness out of your heart and put it into the other fellow's mind and heart."
Charles H. Burr

2. PRACTICAL ADVICE-GIVING BY MENTORS

When evaluating advice, it may be wise to "consider the source." Does the advice-giver know what he is talking about? Chris and Glen were pleased when the suggestions and comments from Norm and Bonnie were not dogmatic, theoretical, or lifted straight from a textbook. Chris and Glen felt reassured by the prior experiences of the mentoring couple in dealing with similar and even more challenging problems from their own special needs children. There is little that adds credibility as quickly as the "they've-been-there" experience. It was obvious to Chris and Glenn that Norm and Bonnie were a valuable source of advice.

3. HEALTHY VENTING OF EMOTIONS

A central purpose of mentoring is to allow candid expression of the strong emotions associated with parenting difficult children. Those who are unfamiliar with troubled, special needs youngsters often dismiss the parents' emotional reactions or are uncomfortable with the depth of frustrations expressed. Unfortunately those most unfamiliar and/or uncomfortable may be friends and extended family members of the adoptive parents. Consequently, in the presence of family and friends, the adoptive parents tend to censor or to skip over their feelings. This produces strong feelings of isolation and the inability to freely communicate (i.e. without sanitizing or worrying about repercussions). Additionally, in meetings with caseworkers, therapists, and other helping professionals, adoptive parents may be concerned about frankly relating how they are doing with the child. They may be apprehensive about voicing feelings of exasperation, fearing that the child might be removed from their care. Further, they may feel reluctant to vent about the system itself, which may be a contributing source of stress for the parents. For these reasons, adoptive parents may find the most non-threatening arena for communication lies in the mentoring relationship.

4. REHEARSING "PREDICTABLE CRISES"

☛ "Failing to plan is planning to fail."
Benjamin Franklin

There is an old expression, "I don't mind surprises, if I'm ready for them." Contradictory as that statement is, it points to a common fact that preparing in advance for the surprises and crises which disturbed children experience often reduces their negative impact. That is why pro-active rehearsing rather than simple reaction is the name of the game. If mentors forewarn and coach mentees about what to look for, and how to respond to key "predictable crises," it may mute the shock and permit a more measured response. Case in point, sexually provocative behavior, e.g. seductive overtures from the previously victimized child, often alarms new adoptive parents and catches them off-guard. Stunned, these parents react in a less than therapeutic manner. Forewarning and rehearsing by experienced mentors allows more proactive, measured, therapeutic responses.

5. EMOTIONAL REWARDS FOR THE MENTORS

From the perspective of the mentors, it is rewarding to offer others the hard-won expertise, the collected experience, and the specialized parental acumen they have aquired. It allows them the opportunity to communicate their interest and to pass on practical knowledge to others (e.g. the mentees) who are happy to receive the information.

"Listening is a form of accepting."
Stella Terrill Mann

6. ENGENDERING HOPE IN NEW FAMILIES

Many adoptive families with challenging children ask, sometimes desperately, "How will this turn out? Is this child manageable? Have we taken on a child who is beyond help...our help? How much danger are we in with this child? Is there hope for him...for us?"

It is very important for new families to hear the message that others have survived. Mentors who have traveled through the dark night of the soul and experienced the desparate considerations of conceding defeat can offer real perspective and instill hope in these new families.

It is very importanat for new families to hear the hopeful message that others have survived and sometimes eventually thrived.

So valuable, then, are mentors who have traveled through the "dark night of the soul" and faced down desperate consideration of conceding defeat. Newly adopting parents need to hear that there can be positive outcomes, if they can endure. Mentoring may help renew enthusiasm and bolster the confidence of these parents, enabling them to "give it one more try," and to endure with their children–to "keep hope alive."